i can
CROSS STiTCH

Elizabeth Spurlock

Annie's® *I Can Cross Stitch* is published by Annie's, 306 East Parr Road, Berne, IN 46711. Printed in USA. Copyright © 2014 Annie's. All rights reserved.
This publication may not be reproduced in part or in whole without written permission from the publisher.

ISBN: 978-1-57367-449-2
1 2 3 4 5 6 7 8 9

Dream Box,
Page 10

Itty-Bitty Memo Board
Page 14

Table of Contents

Woodland Trio,
Page 20

Flower Power Pillow,
Page 40

Birdsong Tote,
Page 34

Introduction

Creating a cross-stitch masterpiece is easy and fun. You can create beautiful, colorful designs to hang on your walls, display on your favorite tote bag, or give as gifts to friends.

We have carefully selected designs that can be framed in a simple embroidery hoop, worn or even used to decorate your room. You can use the colors we suggest, or you can change it up and use colors that work in your room or your favorite colors.

In this book, you will learn the basic techniques to creating beautiful projects simply by making a stitch shaped like an X, and how to finish those stitched projects to make one-of-a-kind pieces. Use these charts and instructions over and over to create gifts for your friends and family or just to add color to almost anything your heart desires. Show off your talents and your creations with confidence!

Meet Elizabeth Spurlock

Born into a crafty family, Elizabeth Spurlock learned crafts from family and friends, including embroidery from her grandmother and cross stitch from a college friend. She has worked as a full-time designer for a cross-stitch publication, and has served as the design director for two other craft publishers. She has also worked as a freelance designer. Elizabeth especially enjoys teaching beginning stitchers and introducing them to the fun and sense of accomplishment that comes from creating cross-stitched accessories for themselves and gifts for their friends and family. She believes that beautiful, fun designs can be crafted even at a basic skill level, and that beginners will feel a greater sense of accomplishment and gain more lasting interest in the craft if they can create something they are proud to show off or give as a gift. Elizabeth lives in Atlanta, Ga., with her husband and two sons.

i can CROSS STITCH

How to Cross Stitch

Use the information in this section to help you create the right stitch and select the correct tools to complete your projects.

WORKING FROM CHARTED DESIGNS

Each square on a chart corresponds to a space for a cross stitch on the stitching surface. The symbol in a square shows the floss color to be used for the stitch. The width and height for the design stitch area are given in number of stitches and in inches; centers are shown by arrows at bottom and right-hand side of chart. Locations of backstitches are shown by heavy lines.

FABRICS

In our materials listings, we give fabric suggestions that will complement each design. Our stitched samples were worked on 14-count Aida and 14-count perforated paper, which have 14 squares per inch; that number is called the thread count.

FLOSS

All of our samples were stitched using DMC six-strand embroidery floss. Color numbers are given for floss. Cut floss into comfortable working lengths; we suggest about 12–18 inches. When separating the strands, gently pull apart the strands and regroup as indicated by pattern.

t!p

You can change the colors to match your favorites or your room. Just select a new set of colors, making sure that you choose the same number of colors, and get started!

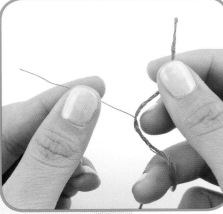

NEEDLES

A blunt-tipped tapestry needle, size 24, is used for stitching on most 14-count fabrics and papers. The correct-size needle is easy to thread with the amount of floss required, but is not so large that it will distort the holes in the fabric. When threading needle, insert one end of strand or strands of floss and pull through.

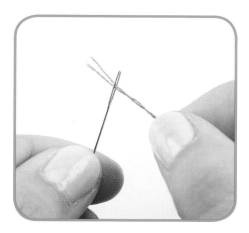

HOOPS & Q-SNAPS

A hoop or Q-Snap, which is a square fabric holder, is used to keep fabric pulled taut when stitching. Always use a hoop that is comfortable to hold while working and will be right for the project. If using a hoop, take care not to tighten hoop too much or it will distort stitches. Center project fabric in hoop or Q-Snap and lock in place by tightening the top screen on a hoop or snapping sides down on a Q-Snap; adjust placement as necessary or when stitching a different area. Never use a hoop or Q-Snap on perforated paper.

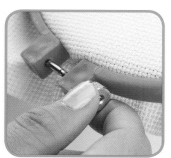

Front of hooped
Aida fabric

Back of hooped
Aida fabric

SCISSORS

Good scissors are a necessity for stitching and are used to cut fabric and floss. Always be careful when using sharp scissors or when trimming your designs; ask an adult for help when using sharp scissors.

IRON

You can remove the wrinkles caused by your hoop by gently ironing the fabric around your stitched piece. An iron is also needed when you adhere your stitched piece to something like a bag or pillow, and you will use iron-on fusible interfacing to do that (see page 36 for more instructions).

Remember to always protect your work by placing a press cloth between the iron and your stitched piece. Never iron perforated paper, and ask an adult for help when ironing.

THE STITCHES

The number of strands of floss used for stitching will be determined by the thread count of the fabric used and the pattern. Refer to the chart and instructions to determine the number of strands used for cross stitches or backstitches.

GETTING STARTED

To begin in an unstitched area, bring threaded needle from back through to front of fabric. Hold about ¼ inch of the end of the thread against the back, and then secure it in place by catching it in the back loops of your first few stitches (Photos 1–8).

Start stitching in the center of a project as indicated by arrows on charts.

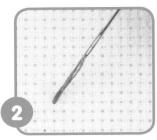

Bring threaded needle from back to front of fabric, leaving at least a ½" tail on back. (Front view of hooped work.)

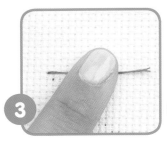

Hold thread tail against back of work. (Back view of hooped work.)

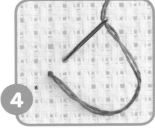

Make first leg of stitch to begin "catching" tail on back of work. (Front view of hooped work.)

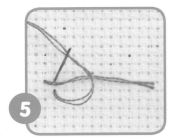

Begin second leg of stitch while "catching" tail on back of work. (Back view of hooped work.)

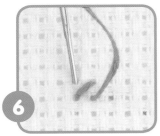

Second leg of stitch. (Front view of hooped work.)

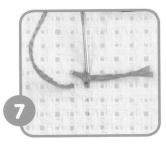

Second leg of stitch. (Back view of hooped work)

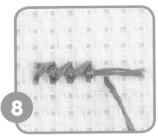

Three stitches worked and tail secured. (Back view of hooped work)

To end threads and begin new ones next to existing stitches, weave through the backs of several stitches. Whenever possible, start stitching in the center of a project as indicated by arrows on charts.

CROSS STITCH

A cross stitch is formed in two motions. Following the numbering in Photos 9–14 below, bring needle up at 1, down at 2, up at 3 and down at 4 to complete the stitch. Work horizontal rows of stitches wherever possible.

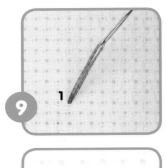

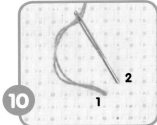

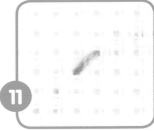

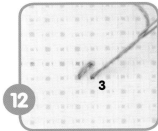

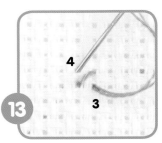

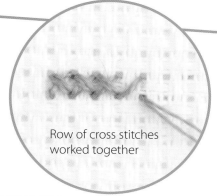

Row of cross stitches worked together

BACKSTITCH

Backstitches are worked after cross stitches have been completed. They may lie in any direction and are occasionally worked over more than one square of fabric. Following Photos 15–17 below, bring needle up at 1 and down at 2 to create one backstitch. Refer to Photos 18–20 for multiple backstitches.

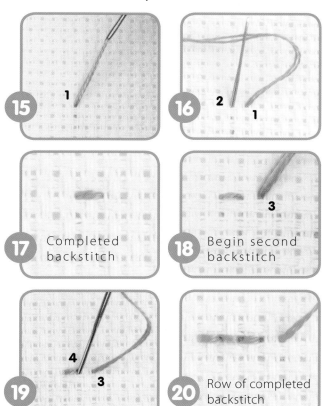

15 — 1

16 — 2, 1

17 — Completed backstitch

18 — Begin second backstitch 3

19 — 4, 3

20 — Row of completed backstitch

FINISHING A THREAD:

After working the desired area of a specific color or when running out of thread, it is important to "lock" your thread before trimming the ends and starting with a new thread. Stop working your stitches when there is approximately 2"–3" of thread remaining. Bring needle to the back of the project; thread through back side of existing stitches (try to go

through 4–5 stitches (Photos 21). Pull thread through snugly but do not snatch (Photos 22). Carefully pass needle back through last two stitches in the row and pull firmly again. Clip ends. (Photos 23).

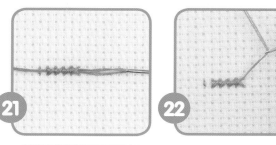

21

22

23

PLANNING A PROJECT

Before you stitch, decide how large to cut fabric. Determine the stitched design size and then allow enough additional fabric around the design plus 4–6 inches more on each side for use in finishing and mounting if finishing differently than indicated. Try to allow 6 inches on fabric and 4 inches on perforated paper.

Cut your fabric right along the holes of the fabric. Some raveling may occur as you handle the fabric. To minimize raveling along the raw edges, use masking tape over the raw edges of fabric, which you can cut away when you are finished.

BEFORE STARTING A PROJECT

- Gather all of your supplies—fabric, floss, needles, scissors, hoop and pattern.
- Wash your hands and dry them really well.
- Hoop or Q-Snap your prepared fabric.

FINISHING NEEDLEWORK

When you have finished stitching, carefully examine your stitched design. Make sure all thread ends are well anchored and clipped closely. If there are any stains on the stitched design, spot clean carefully with water and a tiny bit of mild soap. Proceed with finishing directions.

Lesson 1
Floral Flair

Jazz up any backpack, bookbag or purse with this Floral Flair design. Only four colors are used, which makes this an ideal first cross-stitch project.

MATERIALS
- 7" x 7" piece 14-count white Aida from Wichelt Imports Inc.
- One skein each DMC® six-strand embroidery floss*
- Size 24 tapestry needle

Refer to color code.

DMC®
- ♥ 602 cranberry, med.
- · 605 cranberry, vy. lt.
- ╱ 743 yellow, med.
- @ 807 peacock blue

STITCH COUNT: 21H x 21W
DESIGN SIZE: 1½" x 1½"

INSTRUCTIONS: Cross stitch over one square using two strands of floss.

FLORAL FLAIR

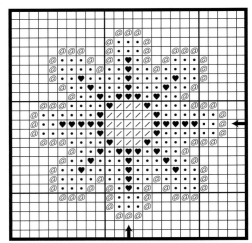

FINISHING MATERIALS & INSTRUCTIONS:
2" x 2" fuchsia felt
White craft glue
Pin back

Press stitched piece from reverse side, straightening as much as possible. Trim stitched design to one square from stitching on all sides. Center flower on felt square and glue in place; allow to dry completely. Glue pin back to center on back of felt; allow to dry completely. ●

t!p

Add your Floral Flair to any backpack or tote bag! You can also pin it to a jacket or sweater for added pizzazz to any outfit.

Lesson 2
Dream Box

Follow · your · dreams

You can never have too many places to store treasures and trinkets, so this pretty box is perfect for a dresser or bedside table. Get creative with your paint and ribbon colors and make the box your own. Make one for your best friend too.

MATERIALS
- 6" x 7" piece 14-count white perforated paper from Wichelt Imports Inc.
- One skein each DMC® six-strand embroidery floss*
- Size 24 tapestry needle

Refer to color code.

DMC®
#	600	cranberry, vy. dk.
♡	603	cranberry
·	605	cranberry, vy. lt.
○	743	yellow, med.
■	3834	grape, dk.
@	3835	grape, med.
/	3836	grape, lt.

STITCH COUNT: 33H x 49W
DESIGN SIZE: 2⅜" x 3½"

INSTRUCTIONS: Cross stitch over one square using two strands of floss.

FINISHING MATERIALS & INSTRUCTIONS:
3½" x 4¾" x 3½" unfinished wood box
Antique white craft paint
Paintbrush
9" x 12" sheet coordinating scrapbook paper
Glue stick
18" length 1½"-wide coordinating ribbon
White craft glue

Trim stitched piece to one square from stitching on sides except in curves and center; see photo for details.

Paint box using craft paint; allow to dry completely; add a second coat if desired and allow to dry. Using box bottom as a template, cut scrapbook paper to size and glue in bottom of box. Using box top as a template, cut scrapbook paper to size and glue in top of box lid.

Glue one end of ribbon at middle of box back; wrap ribbon around box and trim ribbon to fit. Glue remaining end in place using craft glue.

Position stitched design on box lid top and glue in place using glue stick. Decorate box lid as desired. ●

i can CROSS STITCH

DREAM BOX

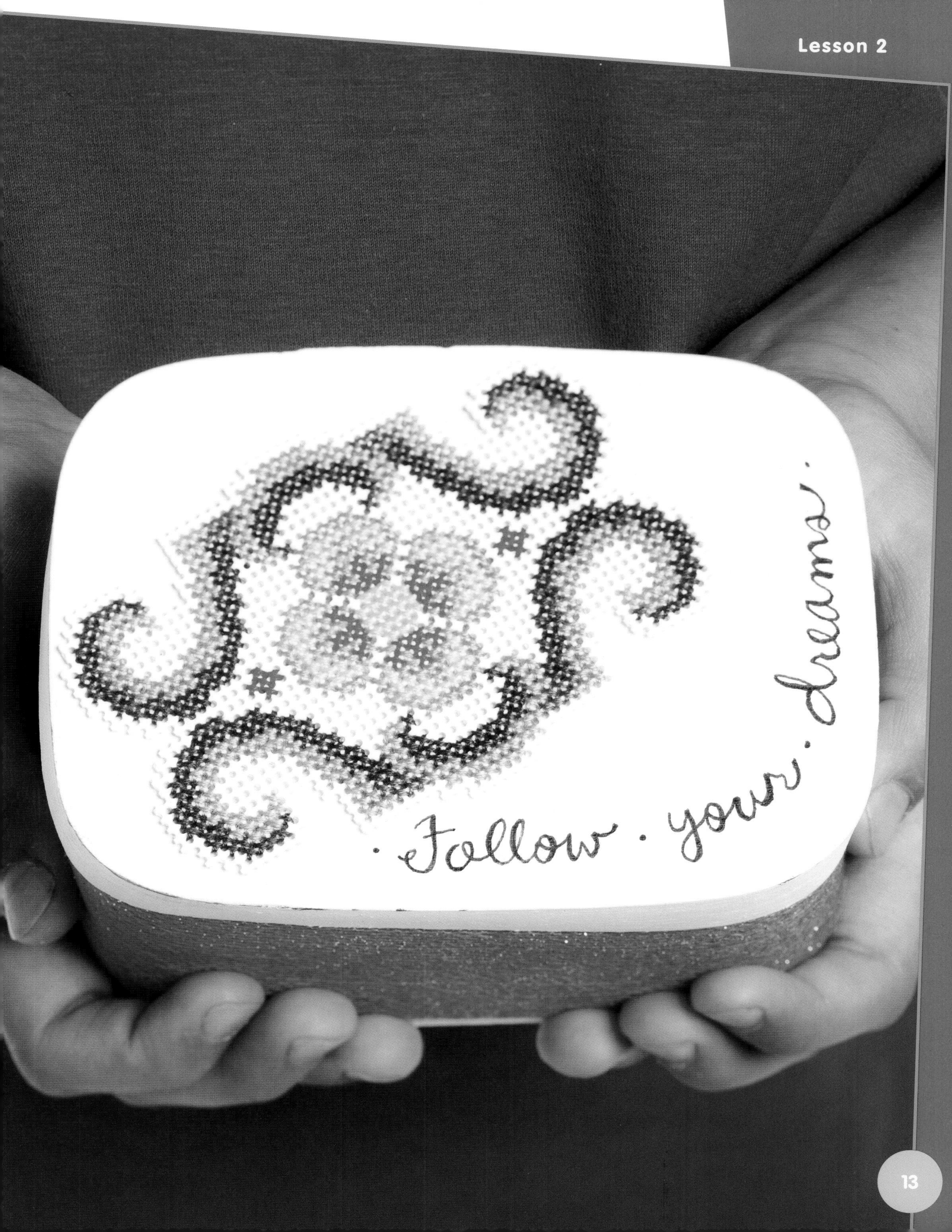
· Follow · your · dreams ·

i can CROSS STITCH

Lesson 3
Itty-Bitty Memo Board

Keep track of photos, notes and schedules on this adorable memo board. Fun little critters will hold important papers in place while teaching you to add backstitch to projects.

MATERIALS
- Five 6" x 6" pieces 14-count white perforated paper from Wichelt Imports Inc.
- One skein each DMC® six-strand embroidery floss*
- Size 24 tapestry needle

Refer to color code.

DMC®
■	310	black
@	602	cranberry, med.
⁄	605	cranberry, vy. lt.
X	666	red, bt.
○	743	yellow, med.
3	907	parrot green, lt.
◑	3765	peacock blue, vy. dk.
·	blanc	white

STITCH COUNT
Ladybug: 11H x 8W
Bee: 12H x 12W
Dragonfly: 15H x 15W
Butterfly: 15H x 15W
Caterpillar: 6H x 13W

DESIGN SIZE
Ladybug: ⁷⁄₈" x ⁵⁄₈"
Bee: ⁷⁄₈" x ⁷⁄₈"
Dragonfly: 1⅛" x 1⅛"
Butterfly: 1⅛" x 1⅛"
Caterpillar: ½" x 1"

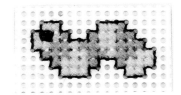

INSTRUCTIONS: Cross stitch over one square using two strands of floss.

Backstitch over one square using one strand 310.

FINISHING MATERIALS & INSTRUCTIONS:

9" x 12" piece coordinating scrapbook paper

Five ½"-diameter self-adhesive magnet circles

Elmer's CraftBond® Extra-Strength Glue Stick

12½" x 12½" metal note board in lime green (KE7807S-LI) from JoAnn Fabric & Crafts

2 yards ¼"-wide white grosgrain ribbon (optional)

Trim stitched design to two squares from stitching on all sides. Cover back of each stitched piece with glue stick and adhere to reverse side of scrapbook paper; trim scrapbook paper along perforated paper edge. Peel backing off one magnet and press in place on scrapbook-paper side of one design. Repeat for remaining magnets and design pieces.

Weave ribbon through holes along memo board edge if desired. Place design pieces in place on memo board. ●

LADYBUG

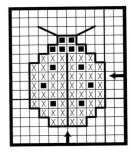

BEE

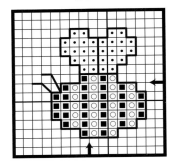

DRAGONFLY

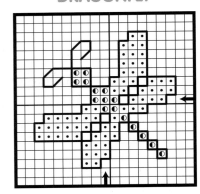

BUTTERFLY

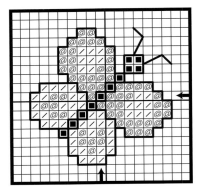

CATERPILLAR

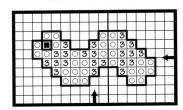

Always ask a parent for assistance when using sharp scissors or the iron.

gymnastics
Lesson
4:30 Tues.

Lesson 4
Polka Dot Explosion

Surround your favorite photo with colorful polka dots with this easy-to-stitch frame design. Stitched on perforated paper, you can easily trim it out and glue your favorite photo in place.

MATERIALS
- 10" x 10" piece 14-count white Aida from Wichelt Imports Inc.
- One skein each DMC® six-strand embroidery floss*
- Size 24 tapestry needle

Refer to color code.

DMC®
@	600	cranberry, vy. dk.
X	602	cranberry, med.
·	605	cranberry, vy. lt.
/	743	yellow, med.
3	807	peacock blue
O	907	parrot green, lt.
◑	970	pumpkin, lt.
■	3835	grape, med.

POLKA DOT EXPLOSION

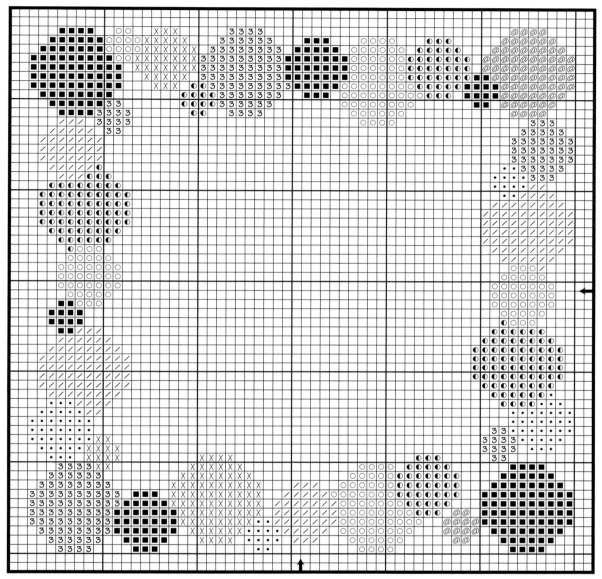

STITCH COUNT: 58H x 58W
DESIGN SIZE: 4¼" x 4¼"

INSTRUCTIONS: Cross stitch over one square using two strands of floss.

FINISHING MATERIALS & INSTRUCTIONS:
Premade white frame with 4½" x 4½" opening
4½" x 4½" piece white cardstock
Glue stick
Repositionable glue dots (optional)

Trim stitched piece to fit opening of frame, centering design. (**Note:** *Stitched model was trimmed to six squares from stitching edges.*) Glue stitched design to white cardstock with wrong sides facing; trim cardstock to match stitched piece. Trim photo to fit within stitched border; glue photo in place or hold in place with removable glue dots. Insert into frame. ●

i can CROSS STITCH

Lesson 5
Woodland Trio

Add a trio of woodland cuties to your room decor with this set. Only cross stitches are used, but colors are carefully blended and shaded to create a trio of adorable furry and feathered friends. Simply finished by gluing them into hoops, these projects will be hanging in no time.

MATERIALS
- Three 9" x 9" pieces 14-count white Aida from Wichelt Imports Inc.
- One skein each DMC® six-strand embroidery floss*
- Size 24 tapestry needle

Refer to color code.

DMC®

@	434	brown, lt.
○	436	tan
♡	470	avocado green, lt.
~	648	beaver gray, lt.
/	739	tan, ul. vy. lt.
☆	743	yellow, med.
ℓ	744	yellow, pl.
◐	801	coffee brown, dk.
✳	807	peacock blue
■	844	beaver gray, ul. dk.
$	907	parrot green, lt.
+	947	burnt orange
3	970	pumpkin, lt.
#	3781	mocha brown, dk.
·	blanc	white

STITCH COUNT
Owl: 52H x 42W
Raccoon: 52H x 43W
Fox: 53H x 45W

DESIGN SIZE:
Owl: 3¾" x 3"
Raccoon: 3¾" x 3⅛"
Fox: 3⅞" x 3¼"

INSTRUCTIONS: Cross stitch over one square using two strands of floss.

FINISHING MATERIALS & INSTRUCTIONS:

Three 5"-diameter wooden hoops
White craft glue
1 yard ⅜"-wide green grosgrain ribbon

Press stitched pieces from reverse side, straightening as much as possible. Unscrew top screw on outer hoop and remove inner hoop. Center one stitched design in inner hoop; position outer hoop in place with screw at top and adjust design as necessary. Tighten top screw to secure hoops together, straightening and adjusting stitched designs as necessary to keep centered.

Carefully trim away excess fabric along back of hoop edge. Apply a small bead of white craft glue to area between outer and inner hoops on back and smooth glue in place with finger; allow to dry completely. Repeat for each hoop and stitched design.

Cut ribbon into three 12" pieces. Thread one length through screw at top of each hoop and knot at top. ●

ican CROSS STITCH

t!p

ALTERNATE FINISHING

Try framing each of the critters in the Woodland Trio design separately, or frame them all together for a different look!

OWL

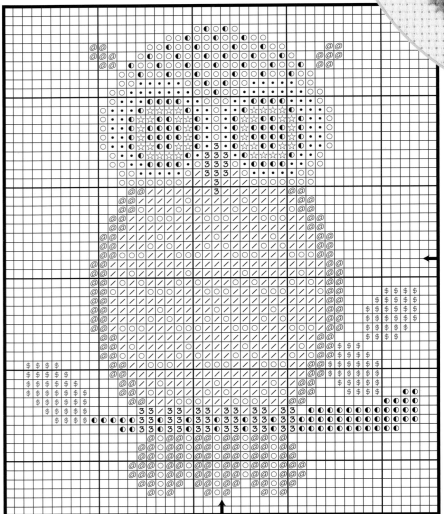

RACCOON

i can CROSS STITCH

tip

Try not to carry your thread across the back of your work. If you are stitching two areas with the same color, but they are apart from each other, always end your thread and start a new one.

FOX

ican CROSS STITCH

Lesson 6
Holiday Jingle

Decorate your family's Christmas tree or give a one-of-a-kind gift to a friend or family member with these cute ornament designs. Whether you stitch the elf, the penguin or both, you will be proud to hang your handiwork for every holiday season.

DMC®

■	310	black
♋	321	red
♡	352	coral, lt.
○	666	red, bt.
∕	741	tangerine, med.
◑	801	coffee brown, dk.
#	815	garnet, med.
X	904	parrot green, vy. dk.
ℓ	905	parrot green, dk.
~	948	peach, vy. lt.
•	blanc	white

STITCH COUNT
Elf: 55H x 50W
Penguin: 57H x 52W

DESIGN SIZE
Elf: 4" x 3⅝"
Penguin: 4⅛" x 3¾"

INSTRUCTIONS: Cross stitch over one square using two strands of floss.

Backstitch over one square for bottom corners of Penguin's eyes using one strand blanc. Backstitch over one square using one strand 310.

BACKSTITCH INSTRUCTIONS
blanc   corners of penguin's eyes
310   remainder of backstitch

FINISHING MATERIALS & INSTRUCTIONS:

9" x 12" piece red glitter felt
Pinking shears
White craft glue
24" length ⅛"-wide white
    satin ribbon
Six ⅜" silver jingle bells

Press stitched piece from reverse side, straightening as much as possible. Carefully trim stitched pieces to ⅛" from backstitched border on all sides and following curve at bottom. Using template on page 28, cut two pieces of felt to size. Center one stitched design on one piece of felt; glue in place. Allow to dry completely. Repeat with remaining piece of felt and stitched design.

Cut ribbon into two 12" lengths. Thread three jingle bells onto one length of ribbon and slide bells to center of ribbon; knot ends of ribbon together. Glue ribbon to back of one ornament, centering knot at top; allow to dry completely. Adjust bells so that they sit atop ornament. Repeat with remaining bells, ribbon and ornament. ●

PENGUIN

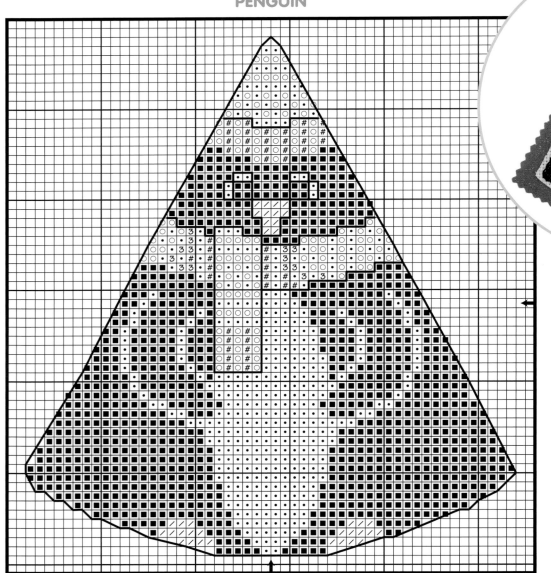

ELF

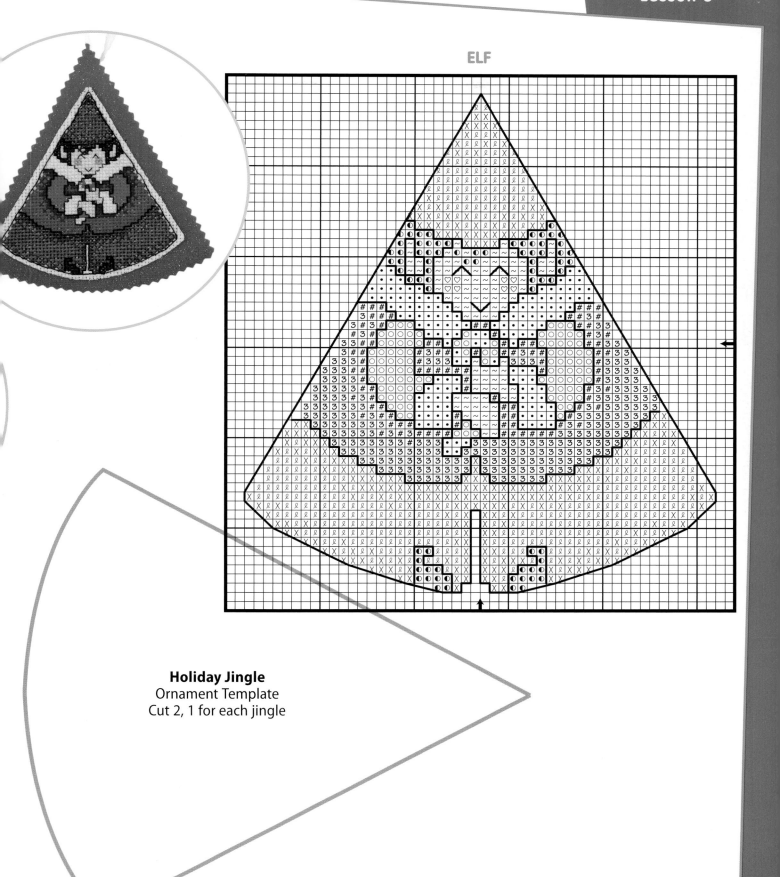

Holiday Jingle
Ornament Template
Cut 2, 1 for each jingle

Lesson 7

Monogram Door Hanger

Personalize your door with this fabulous monogram design surrounded by a rainbow chevron pattern. A simple finishing technique uses cardboard from a cereal box and glue to create this unique beauty.

MATERIALS
- Two 8" x 8" pieces 14-count white Aida from Wichelt Imports Inc.
- One skein each DMC® six-strand embroidery floss*
- Size 24 tapestry needle

Refer to color code.

DMC®
◑	666	red, bt.
○	704	chartreuse, bt.
╱	741	tangerine, med.
·	743	yellow, med.
■	801	coffee brown, dk.
ℓ	807	peacock blue
@	970	pumpkin, lt.
3	3765	peacock blue, vy. dk.
☆	3835	grape, med.

STITCH COUNT: 56H x 56W
DESIGN SIZE: 4" x 4"

INSTRUCTIONS: Cross stitch over one square using two strands of floss. Personalize by stitching desired initial (see page 33), centered in open area in center of door hanger.

FINISHING MATERIALS & INSTRUCTIONS:
Two 4" x 4" pieces thin cardboard (Stitched model uses cardboard from a cereal box.)
5" x 5" piece coordinating cotton fabric
12" length ½"-wide yellow rickrack trim
White craft glue

Press stitched piece from reverse side, straightening as much as possible. Carefully trim stitched piece to ½" from stitching on all sides. Place stitched piece facedown on a tabletop; place one piece of cardboard on back of stitched piece, centering within stitched area. Trim cardboard if necessary to fit within stitched area. Carefully apply glue around edges of cardboard piece and wrap excess Aida fabric to back; press to glue in place. Allow to dry completely.

Place cotton fabric facedown on tabletop; place remaining piece of cardboard on back of cotton fabric. Carefully apply glue around edges of cardboard piece and wrap excess cotton fabric to back; press to glue in place. Allow to dry completely.

Place back piece (cotton fabric) on a tabletop with exposed cardboard facing up. Place one end of yellow rickrack at top left corner and other end of yellow rickrack at top right corner; glue in place. Center and glue cross-stitched front piece to backing with wrong sides facing and aligning edges. Press to adhere; allow to dry completely. ●

MONOGRAM DOOR HANGER

MONOGRAM ALPHABET

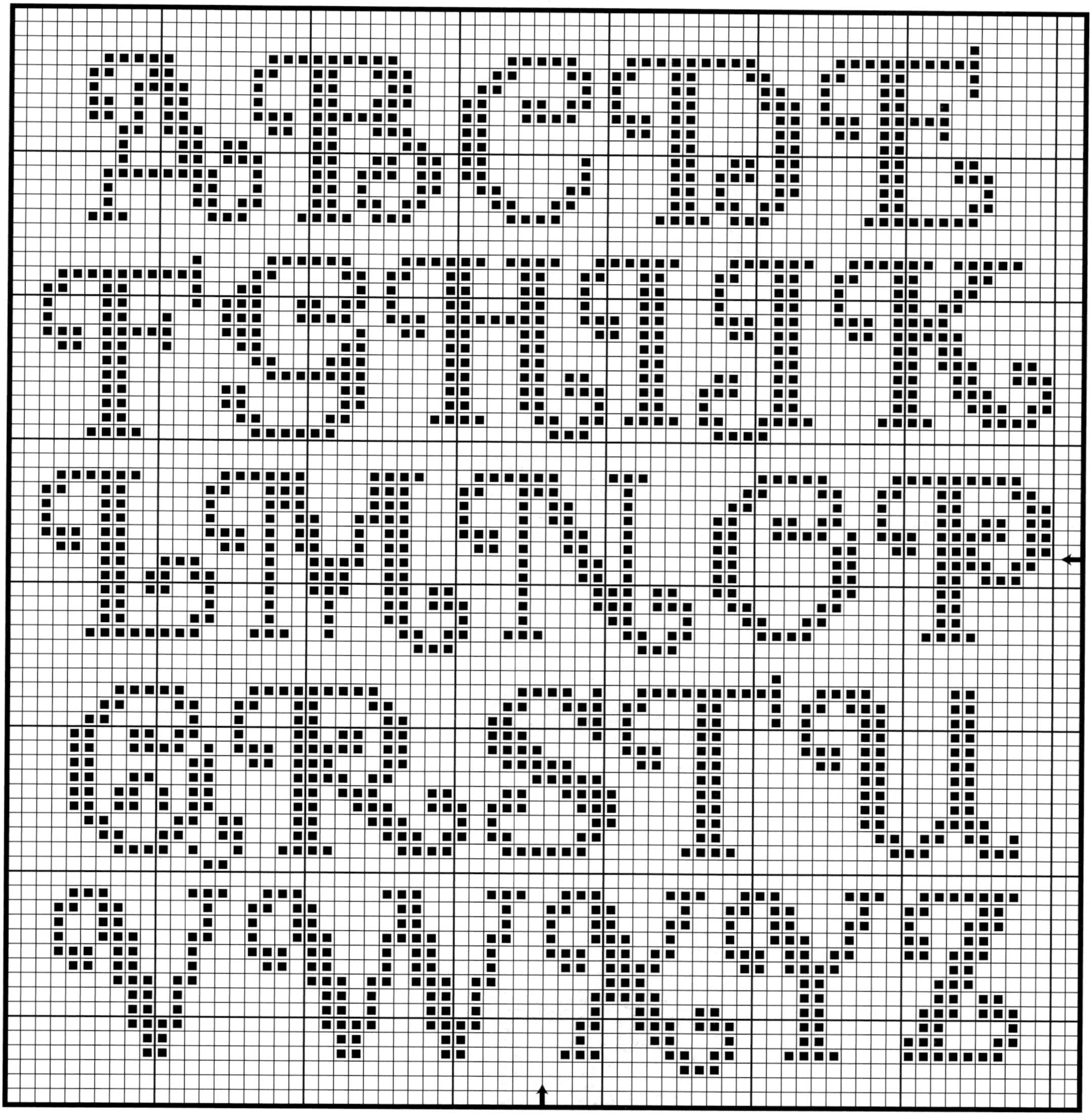

ican CROSS STITCH

Lesson 8
Birdsong Tote

Wow all of your friends with this colorful and fun tote bag featuring a trio of sassy birds in a garden of tall flowers.

MATERIALS
- 13" x 13" piece 14-count white Aida from Wichelt Imports Inc.
- One skein each DMC® six-strand embroidery floss*
- Size 24 tapestry needle

Refer to color code.

DMC®

♥	666	red, bt.
X	741	tangerine, med.
○	743	yellow, med.
•	745	yellow, lt. pl.
@	807	peacock blue
#	817	coral red, vy. dk.
╱	907	parrot green, lt.
3	947	burnt orange
☆	970	pumpkin, lt.
■	3765	peacock blue, vy. dk.

BIRDSONG TOTE

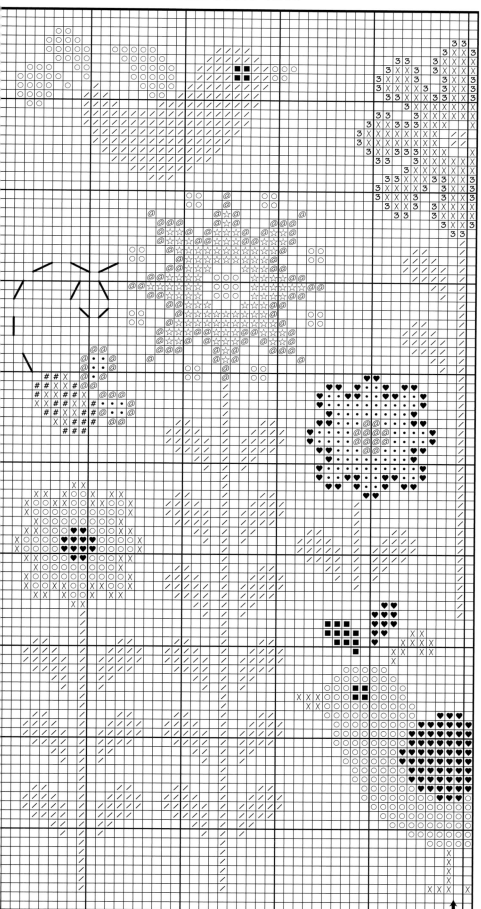

t!p

SPLIT OR DIVIDED CHARTS

Occasionally, a pattern is too large to fit on one page in a book, magazine or leaflet. When this happens, the chart has to be divided into smaller sections. When working these charts, follow directions and work as normal. However, note the shaded area—this is the area of overlap of the two charts. You will only stitch this area once.

Sometimes it's helpful to make a copy of the chart pieces and tape them together to make one large chart.

STITCH COUNT: 95H x 94W
DESIGN SIZE: 6⅞" x 6¾"

INSTRUCTIONS: Cross stitch over one square using two strands of floss.

Backstitch over one or two squares as indicated on chart using one strand 807.

CHART CONTINUED ON PAGE 37.

FINISHING MATERIALS & INSTRUCTIONS:

Prefinished 13" x 13½" denim tote
8" x 8" piece lightweight fusible
    interfacing
Four ⅝"-wide red buttons
DMC blanc floss
15" x 15" piece white muslin or
    cotton (press cloth)

Press stitched piece from reverse side, straightening as much as possible. Trim stitched design to 14 squares from stitching on all sides. Using a tapestry needle, carefully fringe four rows around all sides of stitched design. Center interfacing on reverse side of stitched piece and fuse in place following manufacturer's instructions. Remove backing from interfacing and center design on front of tote bag; fuse in place following manufacturer's instructions and using a press cloth. Refer to step-by-step instructions below. Attach one button in each corner using four strands of floss. ●

1 Using a tapestry needle, carefully remove threads to separate threads of Aida.

2 Carefully pull threads to remove rows of Aida.

3 Center interfacing on reverse side of stitched piece and fuse in place.

4 Remove backing from interfacing.

5 Center design on tote bag front and fuse in place using a press cloth to protect your stitching.

t!p

ALTERNATE FINISHING

Stitch just a bird from the Birdsong Tote and make it into a card for a special friend.

Trim the stitched design to 1 square from stitching on all sides to make a rectangle and glue to white cardstock. Glue bird to a 3" x 3¼" piece of red cardstock. Fold a 5" x 10" piece of blue cardstock in half to create a 5" x 5" card; center red cardstock atop card front and glue in place.

Shaded portion indicates overlap from page 35.

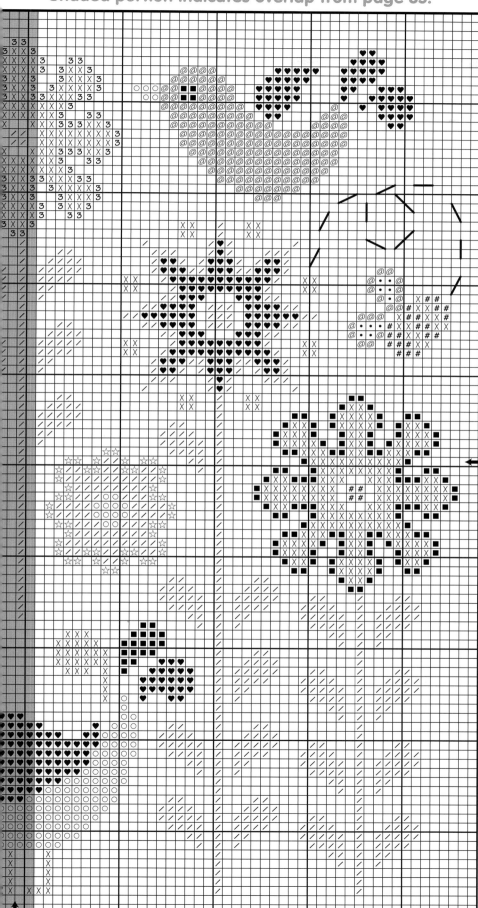

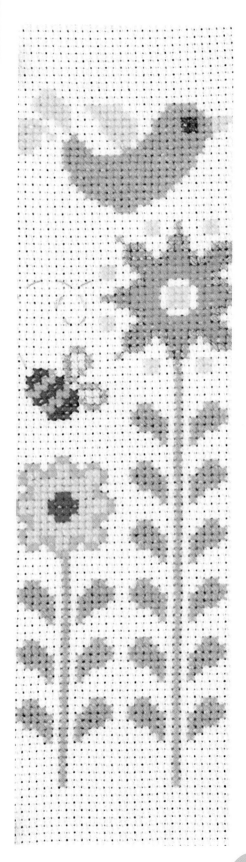

i can CROSS STITCH

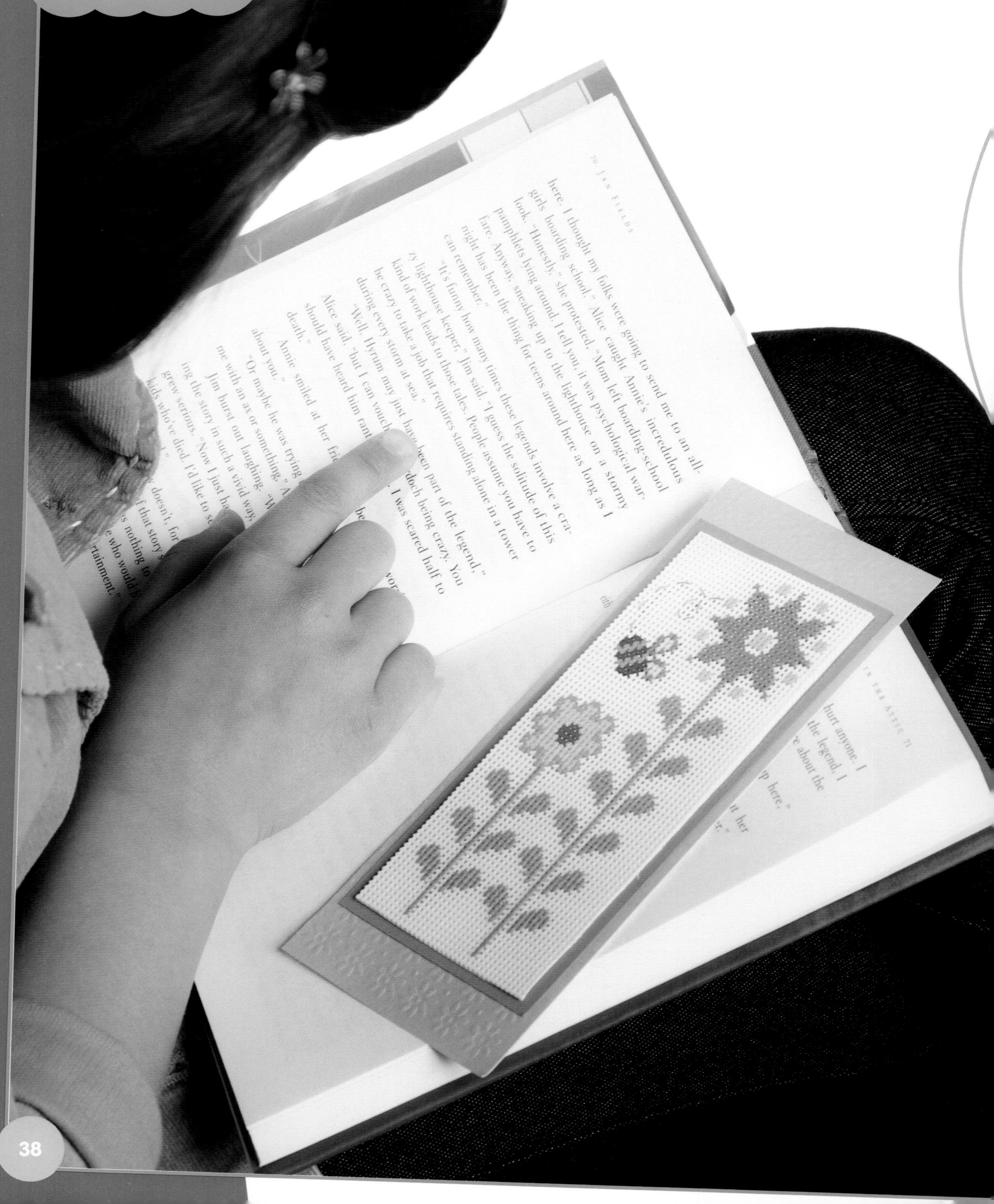

ALTERNATE FINISHING

t!p

How about making a cute bookmark from the flower pair and bee on the left side of the tote design?

Stitch just those things and glue the design to white cardstock. Trim to two squares from stitching on all sides to make a rectangle. Glue it to a 5⅞" x 2⅞" piece of medium green cardstock; center that atop and glue to a 7¼" x 3" piece of light green cardstock.

Lesson 9
Flower Power Pillow

Bring a bouquet of flower power to your room with this fun pillow. This design is bursting with blooms in bright, fun colors. The project is ambitious, so try to stitch one flower at a time.

MATERIALS
- 14" x 14" piece 14-count white Aida from Wichelt Imports Inc.
- One skein each DMC® six-strand embroidery floss*
- Size 24 tapestry needle

Refer to color code.

DMC®

■	600	cranberry, vy. dk.
3	602	cranberry, med.
♡	605	cranberry, vy. lt.
•	743	yellow, med.
@	807	peacock blue
○	907	parrot green, lt.
☆	970	pumpkin, lt.
#	3835	grape, med.
/	3836	grape, lt.

STITCH COUNT: 108H x 108W
DESIGN SIZE: 7¾" x 7¾"

INSTRUCTIONS: Cross stitch over one square using two strands of floss.

FINISHING MATERIALS & INSTRUCTIONS:
Two 22" x 22" pieces white fleece
8¾" x 8¾" piece lightweight fusible interfacing
1½ yards fusible hem tape
1½ yards coordinating 1"-wide grosgrain ribbon
16"-square pillow or pillow form
White sewing thread or white craft glue

FLOWER POWER PILLOW

t!p

When working on a large piece, try not to be overwhelmed. Stitch one area or one flower at a time; complete it and move on to the next flower or leaf area.

Press stitched piece from reverse side, straightening as much as possible. Carefully trim stitched piece to 1" from stitching on all sides. Trim interfacing to fit within trimmed design as needed. Fuse interfacing to wrong side of stitched piece following manufacturer's instructions.

Remove paper backing from interfacing and center stitched design on one piece of fleece; fuse in place, following manufacturer's instructions and using a press cloth. Refer to step-by-step photos on page 36.

Cut two 10" lengths of ribbon and two 11¾" lengths of ribbon. Cut two 10" lengths of hem tape and two 11¾" lengths of hem tape. Align one 10" piece of hem tape along right-hand side of stitched piece; layer one 10" piece of ribbon atop hem tape. Fuse in place following manufacturer's instructions. Repeat for remaining 10" piece of hem tape and ribbon on left-hand side of stitched piece.

CHART CONTINUED ON PAGE 43.

i can CROSS STITCH

t!p

ALTERNATE FINISHING
Would you rather have a wall hanging with your Flower Power design? Easy! Simply center stitched design atop a 10" x 10" artist canvas and pin or staple in place along the back inside edge.

42

Shaded portion indicates overlap from page 41.

Fold under ½" at each end of one 11¾" length of ribbon; press. Repeat for remaining 11¾" length of ribbon. Align one 11¾" piece of hem tape along top edge of stitched piece; layer one 11¾" piece of ribbon atop hem tape with folded ends folded under. Fuse in place following manufacturer's instructions. Repeat for remaining 11¾" piece of hem tape and ribbon along bottom of stitched piece.

Place fleece with design and extra piece of fleece together wrong sides facing. Holding pieces together, cut 3"-long slits 2" apart around perimeter of fleece pieces. Starting at upper right corner, carefully join pillow front and back pieces together by knotting adjacent fringe pieces. Continue around pillow until upper left corner is reached. Insert pillow or pillow form and continue knotting to secure. ●

ican CROSS STITCH

ALTERNATE FINISHING

Impress your friends with a one-of-a-kind headband made from one of the flowers in the Flower Power Pillow design.

Stitch the flower on Aida. With an adult's help, fuse the design to a piece of lightweight interfacing, following manufacturer's instructions and the step-by-step photos on page 36. Then fuse to a piece of coordinating felt (we used white) and trim to one square from the edges on all sides. Attach to a headband using white sewing thread; add a button, if desired, in center and stitch in place.

t!p

ALTERNATE FINISHING
Give a stitched ring to your best
friends by stitching the small flowers
from this design.

Stitch each flower on Aida; glue the design to a
piece of white felt using white craft glue. Trim
to one square from edges on all sides and in
corners. Glue to the head of an adjustable ring.

45

ican CROSS STITCH

Buyer's Guide

The DMC Corp.
(800) 275-4117
www.dmc-usa.com

Wichelt Imports Inc.
(608) 788-4600
www.wichelt.com

The Buyer's Guide listings are provided as a service to our readers and should not be considered an endorsement from this publication.

Special Thanks to Our Stitchers

Michele Byers

Cindy Herman

Michelle Munger

Ann Schmitz

Terri Scott

Connie Winslett

Special Thanks to Our Finisher

Christy Schmitz

10

14

8

18

20

26

30

34

40